The TOPKAPI Palace

SABAHATTİN TÜRKOĞLU

Published and Distributed by:

NET TURİSTİK YAYINLAR A.Ş.

Şifa Hamamı Sok. No. 18/2, 34400 Sultanahmet-İstanbul/Turkey
Tel: (90-212) 516 32 28 - 516 82 61 Fax: (90-212) 516 84 68

236. Sokak No.96/B Funda Apt., 35360 Hatay/İzmir/Turkey
Tel:(90-232) 228 78 51-250 69 22 Fax: (90-232) 250 22 73

Kışla Mah., 54. Sok., İlteray Apt., No.11/A-B, 07040 Antalya/Turkey
Tel: (90-242) 248 93 67 Fax: (90-242) 248 93 68

Eski Kayseri Cad., Dirikoçlar Apt. No.45, 50200 Nevşehir/Turkey
Tel: (90-384) 213 30 89 - 213 46 20 Fax: (90-384) 213 40 36

Translation: **Nükhet Eraslan**
Photographs: **Nadir Ede, Süleyman Kaçar, Haluk Özözlü**
Layout: **Not Ajans**
Typesetting: **AS & 64 Ltd. Şti.**
Colour Seperation: **Asır Matbaacılık Ltd. Şti.**
Printed in Turkey by: **Asır Matbaacılık Ltd. Şti.**

ISBN 975-479-074-4

Contens

ESTABLISHMENT, LOCATION, ENVIRONS 7
BAB-I HÜMAYUN (IMPERIAL GATE) AND THE FIRST COURTYARD 13
BABÜSSELÂM (MIT-GATE) AND THE SECOND COURTYARD 17
THE KITCHENS 22
METAL KITCHEN UTENSILS SECTION 25
THE CHINESE PORCELAINS SECTION 26
JAPANESE PORCELAINS SECTION 30
ISTANBUL GLASSWARE AND PORCELAINS SECTION 32
EUROPEAN PORCELAINS SECTION 34
SILVERWARE SECTION 35
WEAPONS SECTION 37
KUBBEALTI (VIZIER'S COUNCIL HALL) 41
AKAĞALAR KAPISI (GATE OF THE WHITE EUNUCHS) 42
ENDERUN, THE THIRD COURTYARD 46
ARZ ODASI (AUDIENCE HALL) 50
SULTAN'S COSTUMES 52
TREASURY SECTION 55
SULTANS' PORTRAITS 68
CLOCKS 71
(HIRKA-İ SAADET) THE HOLY MANTLE AND SACRED
RELICS SECTION 74
THE LIBRARY OF AHMET III. 82
THE PAVILIONS 85
THE CHIEF PYHSICIAN'S ROOM 91
THE HAREM 92
LIFE IN THE HAREM 104

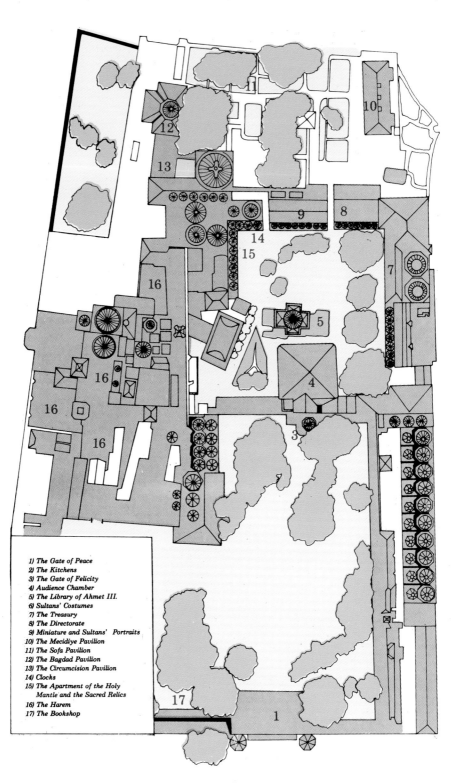

1) The Gate of Peace
2) The Kitchens
3) The Gate of Felicity
4) Audience Chamber
5) The Library of Ahmet III.
6) Sultans' Costumes
7) The Treasury
8) The Directorate
9) Miniature and Sultans' Portraits
10) The Mecidiye Pavilion
11) The Sofa Pavilion
12) The Bagdad Pavilion
13) The Circumcision Pavilion
14) Clocks
15) The Apartment of the Holy
    Mantle and the Sacred Relics
16) The Harem
17) The Bookshop

Plan of the Topkapı Palace.

Bâbü's-Selam, the 2nd Gate.

ESTABLISHMENT, LOCATION, ENVIRONS

The area occupied by the Topkapı Palace extends from Sarayburnu to the Church of St. Sophia. It is surrounded by a high wall called **Sur-i-Sultani** (Imperial Wall) which is fortified with towers and has seven gates. Four of these gates are on the side facing the sea. The most important gate is Bab-ı-Hümayun (Imperial Gate), located behind St. Sophia. It took approximately thirteen years (1465-1478) to complete the construction of the palace, including the wall.

New additions constructed during the reign of each succeeding sultan changed and enlarged the original plan of the palace. The inscriptions pertaining to the construction and the tughras (Imperial signatures) found on the walls of the buildings indicated the reign during which the changes, additions and renovations were made.

The Old Palace, New Palace

After conquering Istanbul, Fatih Sultan Mehmet (The Conqueror) built a palace for himself in Beyazıt, where the university is located today. He lived there for a while and later moved into the palace he had built at Sarayburnu. During his reign, the palace at Beyazıt was called the Old Palace and the one at Sarayburnu, the New Palace.

Originally, a summer palace located by the sea at the tip of Sarayburnu was called Topkapı. After it burned in 1862, the New Palace, in its entirety, came to be known as the Topkapı Palace.

The relocation from the Old palace to the New Palace occurred in stages. First, the government and military offices, then the Harem were moved.

It is said that Hürrem Sultan (Roxelane), one of the wives of Sultan Süleyman (Süleyman the Magnificent), was the first woman to move into the new Harem. Once the Sultan's harem moved completely into the new palace (Topkapı Palace), the old

Mehmet the Conqueror.

palace became the residence of the wives and concubines of the dead sultans.

During the first few years following the conquest of Istanbul, the area where the Topkapı Palace is located today was called the **Olive Grove,** since it was covered with olive trees.

As a matter of fact, Ottoman documents state that Fatih Sultan Mehmet could not find a habitable building belonging to the Byzantine era. However, as scholars indicated and recent discoveries have proved, there are remains of old structures both on the hill and at the foot of the hill. The basement of the building which today houses the Treasury, the Gots column (St. Simeon, 5th century) which stands on the Sarayburnu side and the remains of old structures discovered during excavations carried on both inside the Palace and the Sea of Marmara side prove this. Historians mention the existence of three Greek temples in this area during the time of Theodosius. The one built for the Sun God was converted into a big church (probably St. Sophia) and the other two were also converted into churches. If we consider the Church of St. Irene, located in the first courtyard, we can accept this claim. Undoubtedly, old temples were torn down and new churches, using some of the original materials of the temples, were built at the same site.

The origin of the capital and parts of the colossal column located in front of the kitchens seen after one passes through the second gate Bâbü's-Selam (Gate of Peace) is not known. They belong to the 5th and 6th centuries.

The strategic location of the hill, the aesthetic beauty of the area called the Olive Grove and the view it commands probably constitute the reasons Fatih Sultan Mehmet chose this site to build a new palace. The palace grounds cover an area approximately 600,000 square meters and today only the main buildings are used as a museum. During the Empire, large private gardens of the sultan, vegetable gardens, game fields and pavilions and kiosks covered the rest of the area. Today, Çinili Köşk (Tiled Kiosk) and Sepetçiler Kiosk still stand, and the Has Bahçe (private gardens of the sultans) have been turned into a public park (Gülhane Parkı).

The palace consists of courtyards connected to each other with large gates and the Harem. In the West, it was important to build the gates of a palace on the same axis and monuments were placed on these axes. At Topkapı, however, the gates are not located on an axis nor are there any monuments. Actually, at Topkapı, simplicity and modesty prevail.

The four consecutive courtyards cover an area approximately 370 meters long and 220 meters wide. Bab-ı Hümayun is followed by the first courtyard. Bâbü's-Selam, or the Mid-Gate, is followed by the second courtyard, and Bâbü's-sa'âde or the Akağalar Gate (Gate of the White Eunuchs) leads into the third courtyard. The fourth courtyard, which follows, is also called **Lala Bahçesi** (garden of the male servants in charge of the Sultan's children).

The palace buildings lack a certain unity and uniformity due to many reasons. Each sultan, according to his own taste and to satisfy his needs, ordered the construction of new buildings. The architects who built them had different points of view, used different styles and their personalities, quality of work and education also differed.

The changes and additions made to accommodate the pressing needs turned the palace, especially the Harem, into a disorganized complex. Many changes were made after natural disasters, such as fires and earthquakes. Therefore, rather than a palace, Topkapı today should be viewed as a separate museum of architecture, where different phases of Turkish architecture over the centuries are displayed. The major constructions which took place are as follows:

- Construction of the palace began during the reign of Fatih Sultan Mehmet (1478).
- After the earthquake which historians refer to as the "lesser doomsday," extensive restorations were made during the reign of Beyazıt II (1512).
- After his campaign to Egypt, Yavuz Sultan Selim built the Privy Room to store

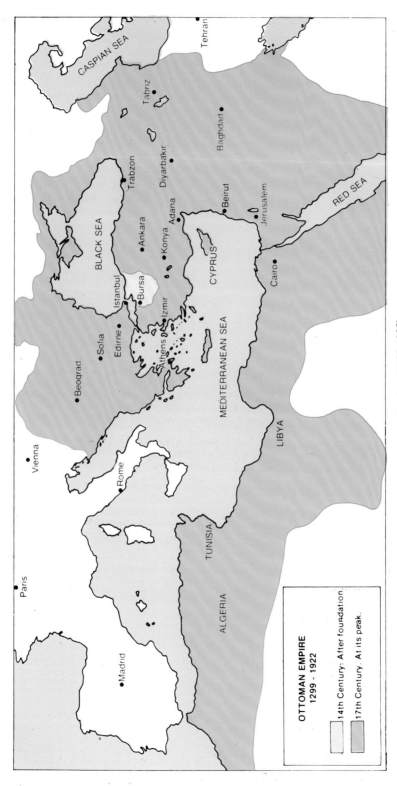

The Ottoman Empire. (1299-1922).

CASPIAN SEA

Tehran

Tabriz

Baghdad

Trabzon

Diyarbakır

RED SEA

Beirut

Jerusalem

BLACK SEA

Ankara

Adana

Konya

CYPRUS

Cairo

Istanbul

Bursa

İzmir

Sofia

Edirne

Athens

Beograd

MEDITERRANEAN SEA

Vienna

LIBYA

Rome

TUNISIA

Paris

ALGERIA

Madrid

OTTOMAN EMPIRE
1299 - 1922

14th Century: After foundation.

17th Century: At its peak.

the sacred relics he brought, and the part of the Harem attached to this room (1512-1520).

- During the reign of Murat III, the kitchens which were ruined by fire, some sections of the Harem and the quarters of the Zülüflü Baltacılar (Halberdiers) were restored (1574-1595).

- After the fire in the Harem, extensive reconstruction was carried on during the reign of Mehmet IV (1648-1687).

- Major additions and restorations, especially in the Harem, were made during the reigns of Mahmut I, Osman III, Abdülhamit II, Selim III and Mahmut II. The inscription plates with tughras indicate that during the reign of Mahmut II many buildings were restored.

The tughras and dates on the inscription plates found on the gates and the walls at various locations of the palace do not necessarily indicate that the particular structure was built or repaired by the named sultan. The inscriptions were changed due to various reasons, or replaced by inscriptions which praised the reigning sultan. In addition, the custom of adding the tughra to The inscription plate was begun after Mahmut II.

A General view of the Topkapı Palace.

The Imperial Gate.

BAB-I HÜMAYUN (IMPERIAL GATE) AND THE FIRST COURTYARD

The **Bab-ı-Hümayun** is the main entrance through the wall surrounding the palace grounds. Located behind St. Sophia, it is the largest and the most important gate of the palace. It was built during the reign of Fatih Sultan Mehmet and restored by Mahmut II and Sultan Abdülaziz. Their tughras are seen on the gate. Every entrance and exit through this gate was accompanied by a ceremony.

Inside, there are rooms on each side for the gate keepers. As we can tell from the old records and miniatures, Fatih Sultan Mehmet had a pavilion built on this gate. It was called the Alay (Procession) Pavilion, but later it collapsed.

The first courtyard is entered via the Imperial Gate. Some of the old buildings housing various services of the palace, such as the administrations of the Imperial estates, hospital, wood depot, lion houses, gunpowder depot and the private bakery located on both sides of the courtyard do not exist anymore. However, St. Irene and Darphane (the mint), located to the left, which were once used as armories, are in good condition. Today, St. Irene, built in the 6th century, is a museum. The jewelry and the gold and silver utensils of the palace were also made in the mint. Deavi Pavilion, one of the most interesting buildings, which does not exist today, was a

The Fountain of Ahmet III.

The Church of Haghia Irene.

small building located on the right, in front of the Mid-Gate. Every day one of the viziers accepted petitions from the public and took them to the Divan (Council of State) to be discussed. Apparently, the first courtyard was open to anyone who had a compaint or wish.

The Admonition Plate and Siyaset Çeşmesi (Fountain of Politics), which was the place of execution, were next to the wall on the right.

The other entrance into the first courtyard is the Gülhane Park Gate, which used to be called the Soğukçeşme Gate. The sultans used to watch the parades from **Alay Pavilion,** built in 1806 on the wall surrounding the palace grounds. It faces Bab-ı-Âli, which was the office of the Grand Vizier.

The wall that stretches along the Sea of Marmara side of the first courtyard was built in this century. The buildings housing various services of the palace were located behind it.

Bab-ı Hümayun. (from M.D'Ohsson).

BABÜSSELÂM (MIT-GATE)
AND THE SECOND COURTYARD

Ioday, **the Mid-Gate is the entrance of the museum.** With **conical capped towers** located on each side and its serrations, this gate resembles medieval castles. As a matter of fact, it is said that after Kanuni Sultan Süleyman's Eastern Europe campaign, the towers were built under the influence of the castles seen during the campaign. Yet, sources indicate the existence of the two towers in the 15th century. The date 1524 is inscribed on its iron door.

Inside the gate, there are rooms for the gate keepers on both sides. In the history of the Topkapı Palace, this area was called **Kapı Arası** (gate courtyard), where viziers and other state leaders were detained before leaving the gate. Actually, there are dark rooms resembling dungeons in the towers. The Grand Viziers used to come on horseback to this gate and then walk in.

Although the outside of the gate has a military look, the side facing the second courtyard is quite charming. There is a wide portico with a decorated ceiling and eaves. The decoration of the eaves are predominately 18th century Baroque. The facade of the gate is decorated with religious inscriptions and tughras of different sultans.

The second courtyard was also called Alay Meydanı (Procession Square). Some of the most important events in the history of the palace and Ottoman Empire took

A holyday ceremony in the second Courtyard. (From M. D'Ohsson, 1790).

place here. Kubbealtı, the building from whence the Ottoman Empire was ruled for four hundred years, is located in this courtyard. The janissaries were paid their salaries (ulufe) and feasts in their honor were given here. Receptions of foreign ambassadors, Ayak Divan (a council held in haste in the sultan's presence), which took place in front of the Akağalar Gate, holiday greetings and other ceremonies, such as paying homage, took place in this courtyard.

An Exterior view of the Kitchens in the 2nd courtyard.

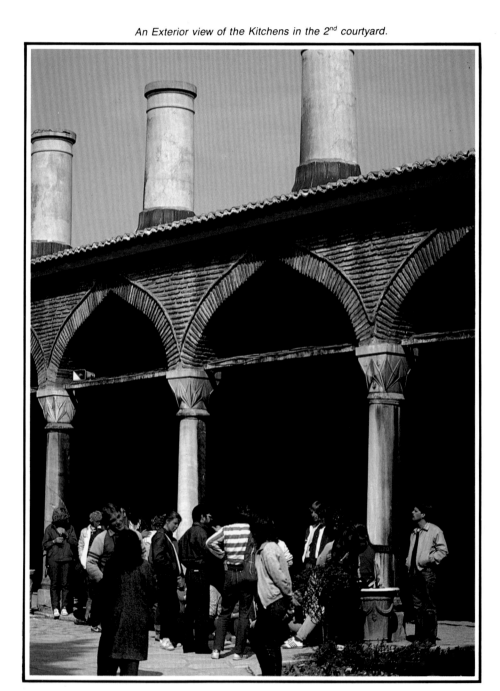

◄———— *The Tower of Justice and Kubbealtı.*

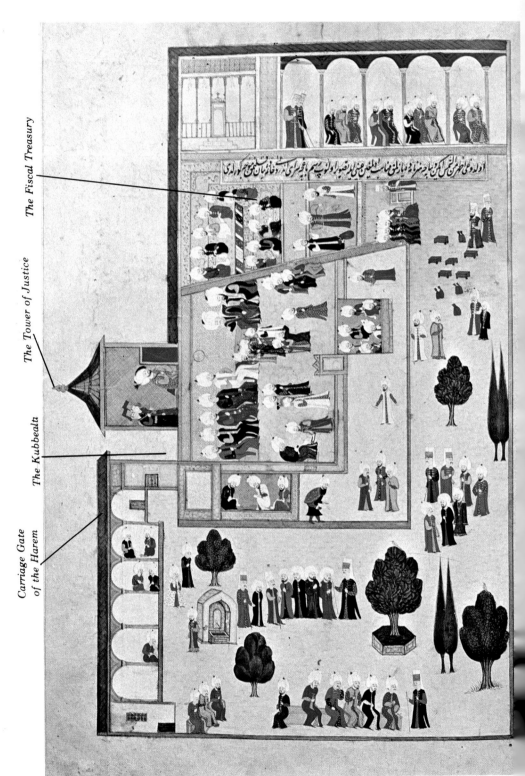

The Fiscal Treasury

The Tower of Justice

The Kubbealtı

Carriage Gate
of the Harem

The second courtyard, Kubbealtı. The second courtyard, Kitchens.

The Gate of the
White Eunuchs

The Kitchens

Bâbü's-Selam

21

A general view of the Kitchens.

Helvahane kapısı. The buildings which housed the kitchens are arranged in a row along both sides of a long street paved with stone. The view is quite picturesque. The two buildings across from the first entrance called the Kileri Amire (The Main Pantry) were the old pantry and the creamery. Today fabrics and **archives** are stored here. The buildings facing these used to be the quarters of the caretakers. It has been renovated and today it is a repair shop used for the maintainance of the museum. As one advances north, the wooden house seen on the Sea of Marmara side is the old **Aşçılar (cooks) Mosque** and the quarters of the cooks used to be across from it. One of these buildings today houses the Silverware and European Porcelains section. Adjacent to the **Aşçılar Mosque** are the palace kitchens where today the Chinese and Japanese porcelains are displayed. After the fire in 1574, the architect (Mimar) Sinan rebuilt these kitchens and enlarged them. The **cylindrical chimneys** are characteristic of that period. A small mosque and **Helvahane** where confectionary was prepared were located at the end of the street and today, Istanbul Glassware and Porcelains are displayed here.

Every day, meals for approximately four thousand people were prepared in these kitchens. Different meals were served to members of the Harem and palace employees.

METAL KITCHEN UTENSILS SECTION

Among the buildings which housed the kitchens, the building where the metal kitchen utensils are displayed is the most interesting, since the giant kettles used to prepare meals for all the members of the palace, service sets and other tools are found here. The rest of these buildings have been turned into exhibit halls, and thus have lost their identity. Cooking pans, copper dishes, bowls, round metal trays, copper jugs with handles and coffee grinders are embellished with typical Turkish motifs. Some of them have inscriptions indicating the date they were made, storeroom in which they belonged and the name of the donor. Most of these were made from wrought copper embellished by scraping and chiseling techniques.

After the 18th century, tombak (mercury plated/copper) vessels became popular. There are a few Seljuk objects and most of them are mortars.

Thera are only a few candlesticks made in the 15th and 16th centuries and the rest of the objects belong to the 17th, 18th and 19th centuries.

The Kitchens, metal containers.

THE CHINESE PORCELAINS SECTION

In the early years of the Ottoman Empire, traditional copper and baked clay pots were used for food service in the palace, but gold and silver pots and plates became popular later during the prosperous period of the empire.

Toward the middle of the 16th century, the use of imported Chinese porcelainware became a tradition in the palace because Chinese porcelains were durable, elegant and of high quatily, also they were expensive imported ware which could be afforded only by rich people and palaces of prosperous countries of the world, like the Ottoman Empire, and there was a rumor that **Celadon Porcelainware** had the capacity to expose poisoned food!

The number of Chinese porcelainware which came to the palace in various ways is over ten thousand. Due to the number and variety of these Chinese porcelains at the Topkapı Palace, this collection is among the few in the world.

Blue-Whites, 15th century.

Even though Chinese pottery dates back to 1500 B.C., it started gaining fame during the 5th dynasty and later became a major export product. Middle Eastern countries were the first to import these porcelains in the 10th century. As a matter of fact, the oldest Chinese porcelainware found at the palace were made in the 10th century. These first came to the palace, not from China, but from other Middle Eastern countries where Chinese porcelains were imported. Records indicate that Yavuz Sultan Selim, after seeing the high quatiy of these porcelains during his campaign to Egypt and Iran, brought them to the Topkapı Palace and most of the succeeding sultans continued to import them. European countries were introduced to these porcelains much later.

The Chinese porcelainware at the palace can be divided into four groups accoring to the Chinese dynasties:

A cobalt blue pitcher and bowl. (Ming Dynasty).

The Song Dynasty (960-1279) porcelains.
The Yuan Dynasty (1280-1368) porcelains.
The Ming Dynasty (1368-1644) porcelains.
The Ch'ing Dynasty (1644-1912) porcelains.
and also according to technique as:
- Celadons
- Blue and white porcelains
- Monochrome porcelains
- Polychrome porcelains

The productions during the **Song Dynasty** were unsurpassed in quality, quantity and variety.

Since Celadons were shipped from the port of Martaban in Burma, they are called **Martabani** by the Turks. There is an impressive number of them in the palace. They are famous for their pale green color, hard glaze and thickness. Celadons were decorated usually with dragon and fish motifs, but plant motifs and geometric designs in relief were also used. There are celadon plates, pitchers, vases and cups.

Cobalt, which is used to color porcelain blue, was known in Islamic lands, especially in Iran, back in the 11th century. After importing cobalt, the Chinese achieved great advances in the art of porcelain pottery and as a result the blue and white porcelains were introduced. The method of using cobalt under glaze started in China during the 14th century and continued until the 19th century. The most beautiful ware made in cobalt blue belong to the Yuan and Ming dynasties.

Most of the blue and white porcelains of the collection belong to the Ming period. The Annam (Vietnam) vase with its cylindrical neck and wide belly in quite interesting, since it is dated 1450.

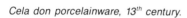

Cela don porcelainware, 13th century.

A Chinese bowl. A censer decorated with metal in Turkish-Ottoman style. (16th century).

During the **Ming Dynasty,** porcelainware was exported in large quantities to European countries, too. In the collection, there are many Large Kraak plates decorated with cartouche designs; plates with rough decorations, small jars with handles, brown or navy blue glazed cups, plates and pitchers which are typical examples of Ming Dynasty porcelains. Also, the white bowls decorated with multi-colored lines and the plain yellow bowls were made during this period.

The porcelainware exported in large quantities to western countries in the 16th century was usually made according to the tastes and specifications of each country. There are some made especially for the Topkapı Palace. On these there are inscriptions written in Arabic and verses from the Koran. Some of these were especially ordered by the Chinese emperors to be presented to the reigning sultan. While viewing the collection certain pitchers, cups and jars studded with jewels and embellished with silver and mercury plated copper, and those with curved handles and caps attract attention. These embellishments were added to these pieces by the palace craftsmen.

The production which had stopped briefly during the Ch'ing dynasty resumed after personal efforts of emperor K'ang-hsi and exports increased again. During this period, the production of the blue and whites continued and two new varities called the **"pink family"** and **"green family,"** due to their color, were introduced.

A plate. (Ming Dynasty)

JAPANESE PORCELAINS SECTION

The Japanese Porcelains found at the Topkapı Palace Museum were made in Japan for export in the 17th and 18th centuries. Since they were shipped from the port of İmari, they are called "Imari Porcelains," There are seven hundred and thirty of these in the museum and they were used for decorative purposes.

Examples of Japanese porcelains. (19th century).

Examples of Japanese porcelains. (19th century).

ISTANBUL GLASSWARE AND PORCELAINS SECTION

Effective production of glass and porcelainware in Turkey began in the 19th century with the personal interest and efforts of the sultans.

Among the objects displayed, those made of glass and Lüleci clay are traditional Turkish crafts. Cigarette holders, mouth pieces for water pipes, coffee cups and saucers, writing sets, etc., made from brown, blue or natural colored Lüleci clay are called **Tophane Crafts** and they were gilded.

Most of the Çeşmi bülbüls (a kind of precious Turkish made glassware decorated with spiral lines), opals, colored glassware, cut glass and crystalware were produced in the workshops located on the Anatolian side of Istanbul. These are known as **Beykoz Crafts** and all of them were produced in the 19th century.

A bowl with a lid, product of Yıldız. The Gate of Salutation of the Topkapı Palace is depicted on it.

The first porcelain factory was established in Beykoz during the reign of Sultan Abdülmecit. The porcelains produced here had the same high quality of porcelains produced in Vienna and Saxony. They were stamped **Eser-i-Istanbul** and carried the **sign of the star and crescent.** The factory produced mainly for the palace and the gifts which sultans presented were made here, too.

After this factory closed down, a new factory was founded on the grounds of the **Yıldız Palace** by Abdülhamit II. **The Yıldız Porcelain Factory,** where both Turkish and foreign designers and craftsmen worked, also produced mainly for the palace. The vases, plates and tea sets produced here are decorated by **Roman** motifs, flowers and landscapes. Some of the tea sets are decorated with the portraits of all the sultans and some carry the tughra of Abdülhamit II. Everything produced here was signed and dated.

19th century Yıldız Porcelainware.

EUROPEAN PORCELAINS SECTION

This is one of the richest collections (five thousand pieces) of the Topkapı Palace Museum. The porcelain factory in Turkey was founded at a time when the palace became interested in European porcelains. Abdülhamit II was personally involved in the establishment of the factory. Even a small museum consisting of European porcelains was established at the Yıldız Palace during his reign. Close poltical relations with France influenced this project. Most of the European porcelains were moved to Topkapı from the Yıldız Palace. Almost all of these were gifts from European countries. The collection consists of German, Viennese and Russian porcelains. They were made in the 18th and 19th centuries.

There are many pieces belonging to different periods of the **Meissen factory of Germany** and the **Berlin Porcelain Factory.** The **Viennese porcelains,** which were made from hard clay, have Chinese style motifs on a red background.

French porcelains, like **Sevre, Limoges,** and **Fountainbleau** occupy an important place among the collection.

Examples of Czechoslovakian **(Bohemian) crystals,** which were the most famous in Europe, as well as **Venetian, Irish, French** crystals and various other glassware are displayed here. These were all given as gifts to the palace.

The technique used in making and the design of these crystals are typically European. Since they were gifts, very few Turkish motifs or shapes were used.

Sevr porcelainware (1816).

A Swedish vase. (1885).

SILVERWARE SECTION

Only a small portion of the three thousand pieces that make up the collection is on display. Silver objects were used extensively in the Ottoman palace. They were made either in the workshops of the palace or at various other workshops in Istanbul and presented to the sultans as gifts. Some were gifts from foreign countries.

The oldest silver object in the collection is a silver bowl which belonged to Kanuni Sultan Süleyman and his tughra is inscribed on the bowl. There are numerous other silver objects in various shapes carrying the tughras of sultans İbrahim, Mehmet IV, Ahmet III, Abdülaziz and Abdülhamit IV. Also, there are many silver objects ordered by the princessess. As a matter of fact, even the European silver objects which have different shapes and ornamentations are stamped.

The gifts presented to Abdülhamit II on the 25th anniversary of his reign occupy an important place in this collection. Models of buildings, monuments, fountains,

Silver model of the Fountain of Ahmed III presented to Abdülhamit on the 25th anniversary of his reign.

etc. made of silver are among these gifts. Example of French, English and Russian-made silver objects are also displayed in this section.

European silver ware, 19ᵗʰ century.

WEAPONS SECTION

The weapons displayed in the building which houses the old treasury are a small portion of a very important collection of the Topkapı Palace.

The main sources of this rich collection are the valuable weapons left behind by the enemy, the weapons made in various workshops in the Empire, especially the ones made in the workshops of the palace, and gifts sent to the palace by foreign rulers.

According to tradition, the sultans and **Turkish leaders** used to store their weapons in the palace. But the oldest weapons came to the palace after Yavuz Sultan Selim's Egyptian campaign. These are very valuable and important from the point of view of the history of the art of weapon-making. Yavuz Sultan Selim brought to the palace the weapons of the kings and commanders he fought and the **swords of the Islamic leaders,** especially the Prophet Mohammed's and the four khalifs', which are invaluable to the Islamic world. Since then, in addition to Turkish arms, many **Arab, Mameluke** and **Persian** arms accumulated in the treasury of the palace.

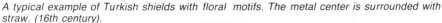

A typical example of Turkish shields with floral motifs. The metal center is surrounded with straw. (16th century).

An Ottoman armor and helmet. (15th century).

Persian, Mameluke and Turkish swords have certain characteristics in common. Originally, they were made straight with two blades. Later, their shapes varied and finally they were made curved with a single blade. Fatih Sultan Mehmet's sword is a good example of a Turkish sword.

The armor has certain common characteristics, too. It is made of mail and reinforced by steel plates to cover the sensitive parts of the body.

Shirts with names of the religious leaders and verses from the Koran written on them were worn under the armor. These names and verses were inscribed on the metal plates of the armor, too. In this section, different shaped helmets, axes, hatchets, bows and arrows and spears belonging to Persians, Mamelukes and Turks are displayed. Even though few in number, European arms, which were either presented to the palace or seized in wars, as well as an Indian shield and Japanese armor are quite interesting.

Turkish Tughras, 17-18th centuries.

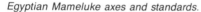

Egyptian Mameluke axes and standards.

Turkish fortress rifles, 18-19th centuries.

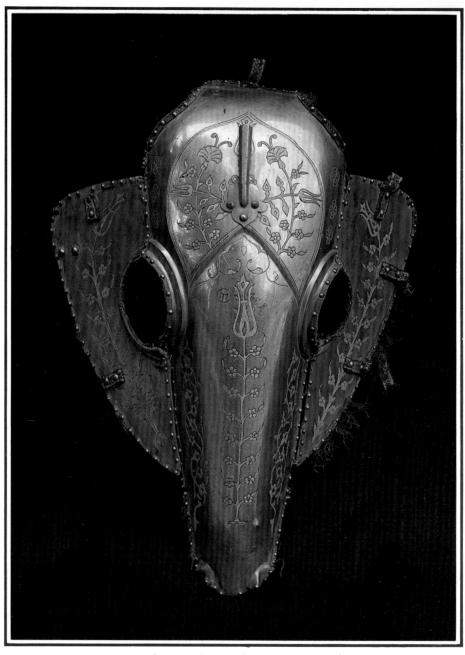

An armor for horse's head. (16th century).

Among the firearms, there are many rifles and guns embellished with ivory and mother-of-pearl inlay and precious metals and jewels. They belong to the 17th, 18th and 19 th centuries.

Very valuable jewelled weapons have been moved to the Treasury Section after the Topkapı Palace became a museum. Weapons of the Prophet Mohammed and religious leaders are displayed at the Sacred Relics Section.

KUBBEALTI (VIZIER'S COUNCIL HALL)

Viziers and other state leaders conducted the affairs of the state and passed resolutions in the Kubbealtı. Therefore, it occupies an important place in the history of the Ottoman Empire. For four hundred years, it was used for the same purpose. It was repaired and modified a few times and acquired its final form and decorations during the reigns of Selim III and Mahmut II.

The Adalet Kulesi (Tower of Justice) is adjacent to the Kubbealtı.Its second story was built in the 19th century. Inside the tower, there is a **window with a grate** which overlooks the Assembly Hall of the Kubbealtı. Until the reign of Kanuni Sultan Süleyman, the sultans presided over the Divan (Council of State). When a commoner intruded into the meeting one day to express his compaints, it was decided that the sultans ought not to attend the meeting. From then on, the sultans watched the meetings from behind this window and the area came to be known as "The resting place of the sultans."

The sultans tapped on the grate and interrupted the meetings whenever they wanted information from the Grand Viziers, who then met the sultans in the Arz Odası (Audience Hall). It is rumored that the members of the council were particularly careful not to make wrong decisions, since they never knew when the sultan might be listening. The Divan discussed the affairs of the state and problems pertaining to the public. After the meetings, viziers used to eat together. The **Divit Odası** (writing room), the section where documents were kept, rest areas and tea rooms were all in the vicinity of the Kubbealtı.

An engraving depicting the reception of an ambassador at the Kubbealtı. (from M. D'Ohsson).

AKAĞALAR KAPISI (GATE OF THE WHITE EUNUCHS)

The third courtyard in entered through the Akağalar Kapısı, which is also known as the Bâbü's-sa'âde (Gate of Felicity) and the Arz Kapısı, since it faces the Arz Odası. It attained its final form during the 18th century. A verse from the Koran and the tughra of Mahmut II are inscribed on the gate and o both sides of the entrance there are inscriptions in the shape of the tughra.

Many important events in the history of the palace and the Ottoman Empire took place in front of this gate. The coronation of the sultans (cülus), paying homage to the sultans (biat), funerals, Ayak Divans, where complaints of the janissaries and public were listened to, holiday greetings,and presentation of the flag to the sultan leaving on a campaign traditionally took place here. Some of the miniatures and paintings depicting these scenes enable us today to get a better idea about these ceremonies The "Protocol Notebook" explains in detail how there ceremonies were performed.

A front view of the Gate of the White Eunuchs.

In front of the Akağalar Gate, Selim III is accepting holyday greetings. (by Constantine of Karadağ).

Undoubtedly, the most important ceremony was the coronation of a new sultan upon the death of the reigning sultan. The funeral, coronation and other ceremonies relating to these events took place on the same day, at the same place, i.e. in front of this gate

Inside, on the left of the corridor with a fireplace was the quarters of the Akağalar (White Eunuchs) and on the right were the quarters of the Bâbü's-sa'âde (The Head White Eunuch), who was the most powerful chief of the palace, and the quarters of other high-ranking chiefs.

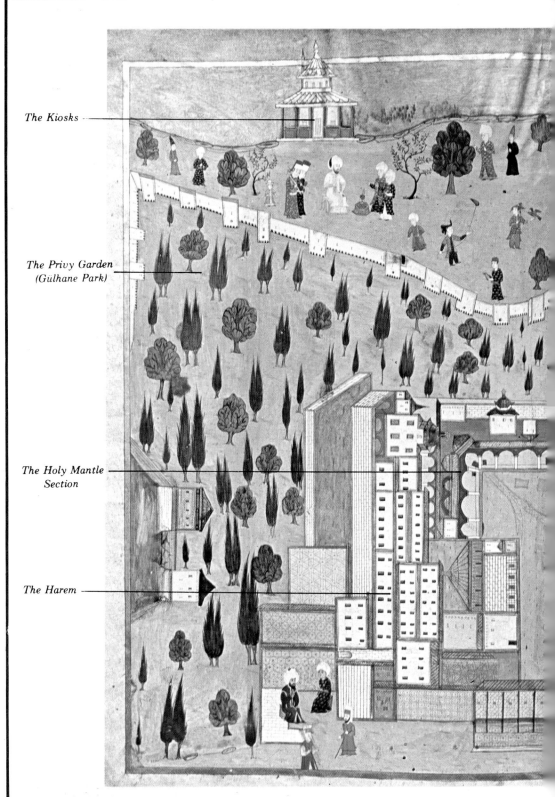

The Kiosks

The Privy Garden
(Gülhane Park)

The Holy Mantle
Section

The Harem

Enderun. (from Hünername, 1584).

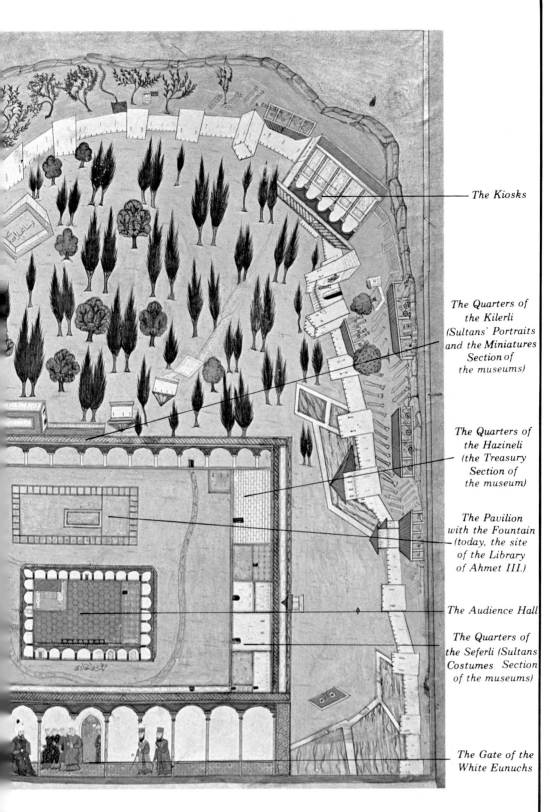

The Kiosks

*The Quarters of
the Kilerli
(Sultans' Portraits
and the Miniatures
Section of
the museums)*

*The Quarters of
the Hazineli
(the Treasury
Section of
the museum)*

*The Pavilion
with the Fountain
(today, the site
of the Library
of Ahmet III.)*

The Audience Hall

*The Quarters of
the Seferli (Sultans
Costumes Section
of the museums)*

*The Gate of the
White Eunuchs*

ARZ ODASI (AUDIENCE HALL)

In front of the Akağalar Gate is the Arz Odası. It is surrounded by a wide eave supported by twenty-two columns. The fountain and tiles on the facade and the marble balustrade give a certain distinction to the structure. Many important ceremonies took place here, too. Inside, there is a **throne with a canopy** where the sultans used to sit and accept foreign ambassadors and high-ranking officials, particularly the Grand Vizier. There are miniatures and engravings depicting these scenes. The ceremonies which took place here followed a certain protocol, too.

The tiles belong to the 15th century and the canopy inside was made by Mehmet III. The inside of the dome of the canopy supported by four spiral grooved columns is covered by lacquered decorations of legendary animal and plant motifs.

The seat of the throne is covered by a jeweled cloth and there are pillows. The sultans' quilted turbans were kept in the built-in closed behind the throne. On the side facing the Library of Ahmet III, there are stairs leading to the courtyard from the portico.

An exterior view of the Audience Hall.

An interior view of the Audience Hall.

The Imperial throne in the Audience Hall.

SULTAN'S COSTUMES

Even though this section is called the Sultans' Costumes, the caftans, which were the traditional outer garments of the sultans, and therefore the Turks, are mostly displayed.

The **Caftan** is a garment which is open in the front and tied at the waist by a belt or a sash. Above the waist, it is closed by buttons or cords. They were worn over under-garments. Some of the caftans on display are lined with fur. Some are made of famous Turkish fabrics like çatma, kemha, sof, etc. The caftan was a style of garment worn by the Turks in Central Asia before they came to Anatolia. They used to be given as gifts to successful state and military leaders. There is a rich folklore associated the this.

Şalvar (baggy trousers), which is another traditional Turkish garment, was worn under the caftan. Trousers were first worn during the reign of Mahmut II (1785-1839), as a result of relations with Europe.

According to an old Turkish tradition which is still practiced today, when the head of a household dies, his clothes are wrapped in a bundle and stored. This is why garments of the sultans are so well preserved. The garments of famous state leaders were wrapped and placed in the mauseoleums built for them. At the Topkapı Palace the garments of all the sultans succeeding Fatih Sultan Mehmet are displayed.

One not only views the garments in this section but also gets a chance to learn about the **famous Turkish fabrics** they are made from. In the inner room connected to the large display hall, there are examples of these fabrics. Woven

An interior view of the Hall of the Sultans' Contumes in the 3rd courtyard.

fabrics like sof, bürümcük and çuha were plain, but silk fabrics like canfes and atlas sometimes had designs.

Turkish fabrics like kemha, çatma (Bursa velvet) and seraser(gold threaded fabric) are well known for their designs which varied over the years.During the 14th and 15th centuries, large designs were used. Toward the end of the 15th century the

A sultan's caftan made of kemha.

designs became smaller, but increased in variety. The Turkish art of weaving advanced remarkably during the 16th and 17th centuries.

In the 14th, 15th and 16th centuries **the motifs used** were originally Central Asian. These were circles inside each other meeting in one point, speckles, Chinese clouds, etc. Later plant motifs like carnations, tulips, curved branches, branches with blossoms, leaves and fruit motifs like pomegranate and apple became predominant.

Unfortunately, the womens' garments were not stored as well as the mens'. Wives and mothers of the sultans left the palace soon after the death of the sultans and their daughters also either left the palace or were married and moved from the palace.

Mehmet the Conqueror's caftan made of çatma.

Süleyman the Magnificent wearing his fur lined caftan.

A caftan made of Çatma.

A "Saz" styled caftan made of kemha, 16th century.

TREASURY SECTION

The pavilion built by Fatih Cultan Mehmet on the remnants of a Byzantine structure was probably the first residence of the Sultan. It later housed the treasury and this tradition continued after the palace became a museum. In the basement of the building a small structure resembling a chapel still exists. When it was built around 1475, the Harem had not been constructed yet. It is not known definitely, but the building was turned into the treasury probably by Sultan Selim. The palace treasury was very rich during his reign. As a matter of fact, for centuries the treasury was sealed by the seal of Yavuz Sultan Selim. It was opened and closed by members of the treasury ward with a ceremony.

There was a bath between the quarters of the Seferli which houses the Sultans' Costumes Section today and the Treasury building. The bath was built by Sultan Selim II. There is a rumor that he died there when his foot slipped and he fell. There is an access from the first hall of the Treasury Section which consists of four halls to this bath.

Only the precious objects decorated with jewels and made of gold and silver are displayed in the Treasury Section. The rest of the objects which had been stored here for centuries have been moved to the appropriate sections after the palace became a museum (Porcelains, Costumes, Clocks, etc.). Also on display here are the precious objects which belong to the **Hırka-i Saadet** (Mantle of the Prophet) Section.

An exterior view of the Treasury Section.

It is necessary to sort the objects found in the Treasury Section, the Sacred Relics Section and other sections of the museum into groups. In each section of the museum, generally, similiar objects are displayed together. Whereas in the Treasury, every object made of gold and silver and possessing jewels, except those made of fabric and leather, are displayed, Among these, household items, kitchen utensils, decorative objects and weapons are the most important. Until recently, even precious fabrics and jeweled harnesses were displayed here.

Until the 15th century, simplicity prevailed at the Ottoman Palace. Gold and silver objects were not used often due to religious beliefs, however, during the prosperous period of the Empire, a splendid lifestyle replaced this custom. The ambassadors and travelers who saw the Topkapı Palace and attended banquets there talked about the grandeur. The jeweled gold and silver table settings were used particularly when ambassadors visited and precious jewelry and garments were worn to exhibit the prosperity.

The objects displayed in the Treasury Section are grouped as follows:
   I. Those made in the workshops of the palace.
   II. Gitfs from foreign dignitaries.
   III. Those brought from conquered lands.

A ceremonial canteen. (16th century).

 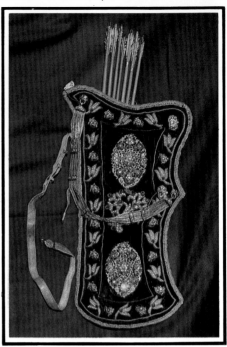

Quivers made of cloth embroidered with gold medalion designs.

IV. Those made in other cities of the Empire and presented to the sultans by Grand Viziers and viziers. Upon the death of the sultan, these were passed on to the palace.

The objects manufactured in the palace workshops were made according to the specifications of the sultans. It is not always possible to place them into particular groups, or to group them according to the technique used in making them. Except for the manuscripts, miniatures and weapons made in the palace, very few objects were signed.

The objects displayed in the Treasury Section are made of metals like gold, silver, zinc, tombak (mercury plated copper) and a few are made of ivory, coral, wood and porcelain. They are embellished with diamonds, emeralds, rubies, pearls and enamel. The techniques used in embellishments were reliefs, openwork, filigree, kalemkâr işi (pen work) and savat (engraving in black on silver), and later applique was introduced. During the 16th century there were more than one hundred jewelers among the group of craftsmen called the Expert Craftsmen.

In the Treasury, there are only a few pieces of jewelry belonging to the women. The tradition of passing the personal belongings of a woman to the treasury upon her death did not exist.

The objects displayed in The Treasury Section are neither grouped nor placed in chronological order. Yet some similiar objects are displayed in the same hall.

In **the First Hall,** most of the objects exhibited are decorated by pearls and made of gold. Various **war weapons,** including armor suits and daggers embellished with precious stones are on display also. These war weapons were used during ceremonies. Zinc vases and bowls, objects made of gold, **a model of a Chinese**

rings, broaches, earrings set with precious stones and three famous and historical diamond pieces are displayed. These are:

- Kevkeb-i Durri
- Şeb Çirağ
- Silahtar Mustafa Pasha Diamond

The Kevkeb-i Durri was made by Sultan Ahmet I for the tomb of the Prophet Mohammed.

The **two solid gold candlesticks,** each weighing forty-nine kilos, were made by Sultan Abdülmecit for the Kaaba. Thousands of diamonds embellish the candlesticks and the tughra of the Sultan is engraved on each candlestick.

The 16th century ceremonial **Holiday Throne** is displayed in this hall. It is covered with old plates and studded with peridots. During the Holy Days, the sultan sat on this throne, which was placed in front of the Akağalar Kapısı. Here, the sultan received holiday greetings. The throne is depicted in some of the miniatures.

The Holyday Throne.

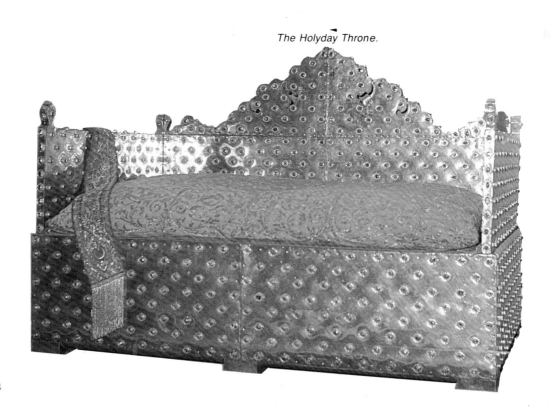

The medals of Abdülhamit and Abdülmecit eras.

Şeb Çirağ and Kevkeb-i Durri diamonds.

SULTANS' PORTRAITS

Portraits of the sultans are displayed in the second story of the building used formerly as the Treasury in Enderun.

The exhibit consists of thirty-seven pieces. Portraits of all the sultans are displayed in chronological order. Other portraits of the sultans, portraits of their women and state leaders are not displayed. Some of the portraits have been in the palace before and others were purchases from other palaces.

Artists of only a few of the portraits are known and many of the portraits are copies of originals. Portraits of Fatih Sultan Mehmet, Orhan Gazi, and Selim II were painted by Italian painters.

Fatih's portrait was painted in 1907 by the palace painter Zorano from the original painting by G.Bellini which is now in the National Gallery in London. Kanuni Sultan Süleyman's portrait is probably a copy of the 16th century original, also.

Portrait of Yavuz Sultan Selim.

Portrait of Süleyman the Magnificent.

Many of the portraits on exhibit are signed by **Constantine of Kapıdağ.** Under the patronage of Selim III, he painted many portraits and pictures including the portraits of Süleyman II, Ahmet II, Mustafa II, Selim III and the scene of a holiday ceremony. The portrait of Abdülaziz was painted by the Polish painter Clobowski. Aivazovsky painted Sultan Murat V's portrait and the Austrian painter Krausz painted Sultan Reşat's portrait.

Murat IV.

Mahmut I.

Ahmet III.

Portrait of Selim III. (By Constantine of Karadağ).

CLOCKS

The clocks are exhibited in the former Treasury of Silahtar (Sword-bearer), located next to the Holy Mantle Section in Enderun courtyard. Although there are about three hundred and fifty clocks in the palace,only half of these are on exhibit and most of them belong to the 18th and 19th centuries.

About thirty of these clocks are Turkish. The rest were either purchased from Europe or presented to the palace as gifts. Clock manufacturing is Istanbul started in the 16th century and the Galata district of Istanbul was the watchmaking center.

The oldest **Turkish-made clocks** belong to the 17th century and there are four of them. Later, clock manufacturing was influenced by English watchmaking and in the 19th century other developments occurred.

Most of the Turkish-made clocks are signed, and therefore, the names of the craftsmen are known. Since they embellished both the cases and dial plates, the clocks are rare example of Turkish jewelry, wood and metal crafts. The majority of the watchmakers in the 19th century were Mevlevis, therefore some of the clocks

Interior of the Clocks Section.

made then are shaped like a Mevlevi headgear, which is a conical cap. The sultan was the patron of the watchmakers.

Most of the clocks are foreign made. In the collection there are many **English,** but also **German, Austrian, French, Swiss** and **Russian** clocks. These were brought by the ambassadors of European heads of state. Since the English clocks were quite popular, many **Markwick-Markham-**brand clocks were imported. Also, in the 18th century many clocks signed **Le Roy** were purchased from France.

As the English and French clocks were made especially for Turkey, the numbers were written in Arabic and some of the clocks were decorated by scenes of Istanbul. Most of them are musical clocks.

English made clock with an organ. (18th century).

Turkish made clock with a wood console.

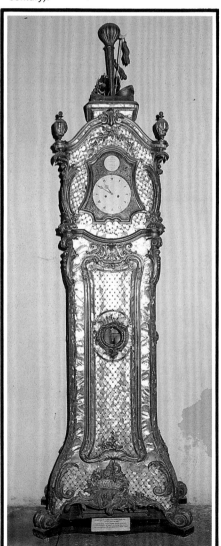

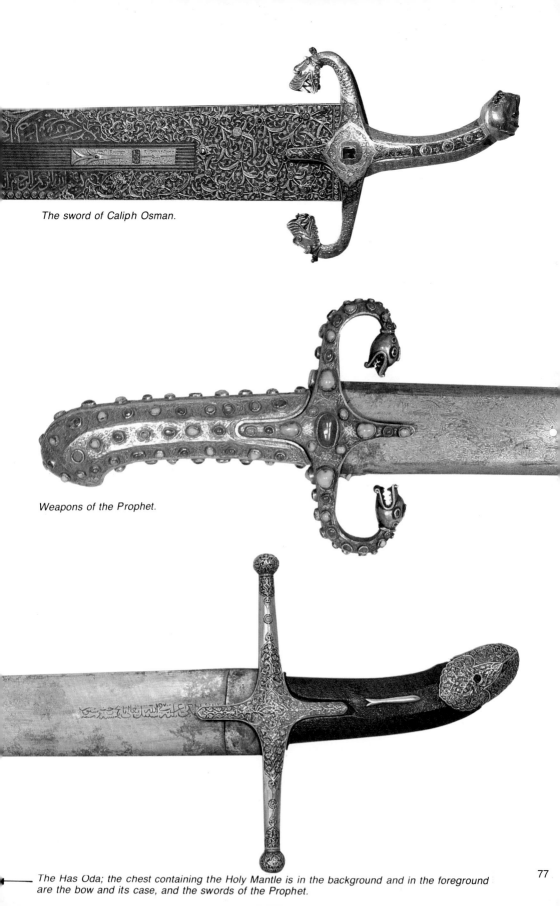

The sword of Caliph Osman.

Weapons of the Prophet.

The Has Oda; the chest containing the Holy Mantle is in the background and in the foreground are the bow and its case, and the swords of the Prophet.

The Seal of The Prophet (Mühr-ü Saadet)

According to historians, the seal of the Prophet was passed first to Caliph Abubakr, then to Omar and then to Osman, who dropped it in a well. The seal displayed in the Holy Mantle Section was discovered in the middle of the 19th century in Baghdad and brought to the Topkapı Palace.

The Tooth of the Prophet (Dendan-ı Saadet)

It is a piece of his tooth, broken during the war of Uhut. It is kept in a gold-decorated case ordered by Sultan Mehmet IV.

The Beard of the Prophet (Lihye-i Saadet)

There are close to sixty hairs of his beard in the Holy Mantle Section. Twenty-four of these are kept in cases decorated with gold and precious stones, or in boxes embellished with mother-of-pearl inlay.

The Footprints of the Prophet (Nakş-ı Kadem-i Şerif)

There are six footprints of the Prophet in the Holy Mantle Section. Some of them appear in stone, some in brick. The stone with his footprint is supposed to be the

The footprint of the Prophet.

Rain gutters from the Kaaba.

A lock belonging to the Kaaba.

The seal of the Prophet.

The Koran read when Caliph Osman died.

stone he stepped on when he ascended into Heaven. It is desplayed in a gold frame with a cover.

The Banner of the Prophet (Sancak-ı Şerif)

Sources indicate that the Prophet used one black and a few white banners, especially during wars. The black banner called Ukap, which supposedly was sent by Hayırbay from Egypt, is kept in a small chest. It was ruined by weather and extensive use. Later, pieces of the banner were sewn over a new banner made of green silk.

Other Sacred Swords (Süyufu Mübâreke)

There are twenty other swords besides the two of the Prophet. Except for the two swords which are assumed to have belonged to the disciples of the Prophet, owners of the other swords are known. Some of the swords were decorated with gold, silver and precious stones after they were brought to the Palace.

The swords and the religious leaders who owned them are listed in chronological order as:

-The Sword of Prophet David
-The Sword of Caliph Abubakr
-The Sword of Caliph Omar
-The Sword of Caliph Osman
-The Sword of Caliph Ali
-The Sword of Companion Zeynel Abidin
-The Sword of Companion Zubeyr Ibn-i al Avam
-The Sword of Ebul Hasan, secretary of the Prophet
-The Sword of Cafer-i Tayyar
-The Sword of Halid bin Velid
-The Sword of Ammar bin Yasir

Besides these, in the Holy Mantle Section, there are objects belonging to the companions of the Prophet and other religious leaders, many **Korans,** among which those attributed to the caliphs Osman and Ali, and **objects from the Kaaba** are found. Old materials left over from restorations done at the Kaaba are displayed also. Most important of these are the **cases of the sacred Black Stone (Hacer-i Esved)** in the Kaaba, **roof gutters, covers** and thirty-four **locks and keys** which have great artistic value.

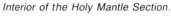

Interior of the Holy Mantle Section.

ورقه گلشه

ستون بالا راست:

نیش خاک بر تیز خاک
بمندق کند از ماه مشک
همی کنت فریاد از این تیره بخت
رهجران برانش فلک دانه تیغ
بزاری سوی آسمان کرد سر
تو دانی که بخت صبر و بی طاقتم
کنون ای سرو را در کنار

ستون بالا چپ:

بمالید بغلتید بر خاک رخسار پاک
بی افکندان سرو بر خاک خشک
کی اوکند برجان من بند سخن
ندانم چه خواهد همی این دم
همی کنت ای داور دادگر
نوده سیدی زین بد زاحم
بیوسید رخساران نو بهار

ستون پایین راست:

بکلشه چنین کنت بدرود باش
همی با نیم زار نالان شدن شدن
همی کنت از غم شده های های
بلی حانم آورد یکی زده
بکل شاه داد ان بخت یاذکار
همی شد بره ورقه زاری کان

ستون پایین چپ:

ازین خسته دل توخشنود باثر
ندانم که چون باشده آمذن
همی راند بیحانه برک همای
لکن پسرنگار وزده پسرکرد
نشست از بر بابه زاهوار
خروشید کلشاه کیسو کنات

THE PAVILIONS

There are three passage ways, (one covered) from the third courtyard, Enderun, into the fourth courtyard. With its beautiful gardens and pavilions built in the corners, the fourth courtyard is more of a recreation area than a regular courtyard. As a matter of fact, the sultans and their families spent most of their time in these gardens and pavilions. Some of the famous merriments of the Tulip Period were staged here. Gardens built at different levels, pavilions expertly placed in corners, pools and fountains in the gardens are **characteristics of the "Fourth Place."**

On the north side of the fourth courtyard, there is a marble-paved terrace ascended by steps. The big **pool with a fountain** in the middle is surrounded by the Revan, Baghdad, and the Sünnet Pavilions and a **baldachin.**

The Pavilions are listed in chronological order as:

THE REVAN PAVILION: It was constructed in 1635 to commemorate Sultan Murat IV's Revan campaign. It has an octagonal floor plan and the interior is decorated with typical 17th century architectural embellishments. The stained glass windows, doors and built-in closet doors decorated with mother-of-pearl and tortoise shell inlay and tiles are worth examining closely. For a while, the pavilion was used as a library.

THE BAGHDAD PAVILION: It was constructed in 1639 by Sultan Murat IV to commemorate his Baghdad campaign. It is the most beautiful and elegant pavilion

An engraving depicting the Baghdad Pavilion and the Pavilion of Mustafa Pasha. (from W. H. Bartlett, 1839).

The Pavilion of Mustafa Pasha.

Interior of the Baghdad Pavilion.

of the Palace. It has an octagonal floor plan also and the north side of the building rests on columns. There are wide eaves all around the building. The walls, both on the inside and outside, are covered with exquisite tiles of the period. The doors are decorated with mother-of-pearl inlay and the stained glass windows are beautiful examples of the creations of Turkish craftsmen. Below the stained glass upper windows, a tile frieze with inscriptions of verses from the Koran encircles the interior. The decorations on the inside of the dome and the geometric designs at its perimeter are rare examples of the Turkish art of embellishment. To the right of the entrance, there is a magnificent gilded-copper fireplace.

THE CIRCUMCISION PAVILION: Also known as the Circumcision Room, it was constructed by Sultan İbrahim I, who succeeded Sultan Murat IV to imitate him. The walls on the south side are covered with exquisite tiles, both inside and outside. The tiles, particularly those on the outside, have interesting blue plant motifs with animal motifs dispersed among them. Inside, there are fountains in the window recesses and a gilded-copper fireplace. It is rumored that the royal princes were circumcised here.

The baldachin overlooking Haliç (The Golden Horn) was also built by Sultan İbrahim I. It is said that the sultans used to break their fast here during Ramadan. There are various verses and prayers from the Koran inscribed both on the interior and exterior of the canopy.

Another view of the interior of the Baghdad Pavilion.

The Baghdad Pavilion.

The pool in front of the Baghdad Pavilion and in the background is the. Sünnet Pavilion.

THE CHIEF PYHSICIAN'S ROOM

Originally, it was built during the reign of Fatih Sultan Mehmet as one of the towers of the wall surrounding the palace grounds. For a long time it was used by the chief physicians of the sultans as a **pharmacy** and office. During the 19th century, it was used as a place **where the Enderun eunuchs practiced music.** For a while, it was used even as a **repair shop for weapons.**

During the reign of Mahmut II, there was a wooden story on top of this tower made of stone, but later it collapsed.

Behind the tower, there is a stone chair where Sultan Murat IV used to sit and watch the games played. Since the chief lalas (man servants in charge of the sultan's children) supervised the chief physicians while they were preparing medicine, this structure is also called **Başlala** (chief Lala) Tower.

Today, only the two stories stand. After it was restored, everything related to medicine and pharmacy stored in the Treasury and other parts of the Palace were brought here, and in 1982, they were put on display. Drugs and pharmaceutical tools are exhibited in the first story. The second story is arranged as the office of the Chief Physician. Besides the tools he used, books and framed inscriptions pertaining to medicine are exhibited.

A medicine bottle and its case.

A birds-eye view of the Harem.

Even though it was known as the Harem, the residence of the sultans and their women was also called **Dar'üs Saade** (House of Felicity).

Not only in the Ottoman Palace, but also in the history of all eastern countries, due to the mystery surrounding it, the word Harem brings to mind the Harem of the Topkapı Palace. How much is know about the Harem which, in western literature, was a very popular subject, often embellished? In reality, due to the ethics of Islam and specific rules of the Harem, only the sultan, his family and a certain group of people in their service could enter the Harem. These restrictions intensified the mystery associated with it. As usual,because of natural curiosity toward anything prohibited, the Harem attracted exteme interest. A lot of fiction has been written about it and imaginary and exaggerated life styles have been accepted as real.

Was it forbidden to describe the private lives of the sultans and their women outside the Harem? There are no documents on the subject and there is no need for it, either. The private lives of all the rulers in the world are secret. What made the Harem so different was the fact that nobody besides the principle employees of the Harem was allowed to enter. Harem means "a place forbidden to enter." Not even the grand viziers, viziers, ambassadors or other palace employees were allowed to enter. Only a few who did not belong to the Harem could enter it. These were the palace physicians, repairmen, piano and organ tuners, etc. What they described did not go beyond the building and furniture. Besides the physicians, nobody saw the women.

All the banquets and receptions for Turkish and foreign statesmen, meetings and audiences with the sultans took place outside the Harem.

The Courtyard of the Valide Sultan.

Although life in the Harem is not known, its organization and the way it functioned were deduced from various documents. Food and wardrobe expenses indicated the number of people in the harem; documents on salaries and appointments gave information about their titles and the charities they were involved with gave an idea about their character. Written documents such as orders, permits and accounts and even the letters let by the sultans and high-ranking officials of the palace enable us to understand the organization and even the life in the Harem.

The Topkapı palace was build by Fatih Sultan Mehmet, but the Harem moved here seventy years later from the Old Palace, located in the Beyazıt district of Istanbul. The date of the construction and the date of the settlement into the Harem are disputed. Sources indicate that Kanuni Sultan Süleyman had the Harem built on the insistence of his wife Roxelane. The relocation of women into the Topkapı Palace took place in phases and it was completed during **the reign of Sultan Murat III,** when the concubines also were finally moved in.

When the succeeding sultans had new buildings added, the Harem now lost its original plan and became a disorganized complex. Every sultan did not live in the Harem. Some lived here periodically, some preferred the palace in Edirne and some lived in private kiosks and palaces they had built by the shores of the Bosphorous or the Golden Horn.

Upon completion of the Dolmabahçe Palace in 1853 the Harem in its entirety was moved there.

Interior of the Imperial Hall. (Hünkâr Sofası).

The Harem; the Hall with a Fountain.

The fountain in Murat III's room.

The Harem of the Topkapı Palace consists of three main sections.
1. The Black Eunuch's section
2. The Women's section
3. The Sultan's section

For all these people there were about three hundred rooms, baths, lavatories, a hospital for the concubines and kitchens. The Harem, which occupies an area as large as a city district, consists of marble **paved courtyards surrounded by porches** and rooms. It is necessary to consider each courtyard and its surroundings as a unit.

From the palace, there are **two entrances** into the Harem: **The Arabalar (Carriage) Gate** and the **Kuşhane (Saucepan) Gate,** where the food was brought in. The traffic through both gates was controlled by the black eunuchs. All the buildings between these two gates were reserved for the various services and as the residences of **the black eunuchs.** They were sent to the palace by governors of Egypt and trained in the Harem under strict discipline. The Chief Black Eunuch was one of the people closest to the sultan, and he was one of the most influential people in the palace after the Grand Vizier.

The entrance located next to the Kubbealtı was originally the entrance to the Quarters of the Black Eunuchs. The women of the Harem used to leave through this gate and get on the carriages.

There are many rumors and legends about the first **room with a closet** located next to this gate. Further on the left is the Mescid (small mosque) of the Black Eunuchs. The walls of the Mescid and the walls facing open and covered courtyards are covered with tiles. On the doors leading into the courtyards, porticos and apartments there are inscriptions praising the sultans, and also **deeds of trust.**

The Harem; the dome of Murat III's room.

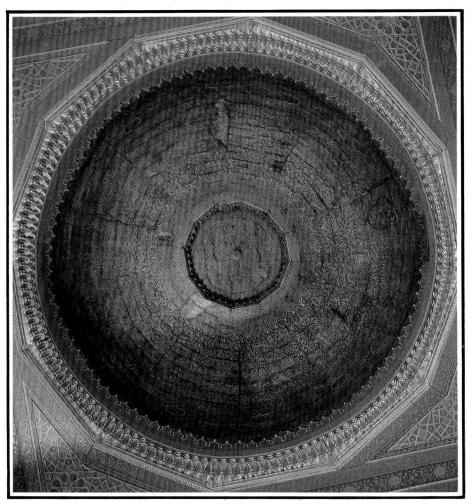

The apartment of the Crown Prince. (Detail of the dome).

typical 16th century structure. Later, in the beginning of the 17th century, Sultan Ahmet I added a **reading room** and Sultan Ahmet III added a dining room. The mother-of-pearl and tortoise shell inlay on the doors of the book cases in the reading room and the wall decorations of the dining room are of very high quality and beautiful examples of the Turkish art of embellishment. Due to the lacquered decorations of fruit motifs on the wood wall panels, the dining room built by Sultan Ahmet III is called the **Fruit Room.** It was supposedly built in 1705.

The location of the bedroom of the sultans has not been established. Sources indicate that a bed and a mosquito net were placed wherever the sultan wanted to spend the night.

In the 17th century, the apartment built by Sultan Murat III was rearranged and the **Apartment of the Crown Prince** was added on to the north of it. This building which consists of two consecutive rooms possesses many characteristics of Turkish architecture. The embellishments on the linen fabric stretched inside the dome, tiles, stained glass windows, and built-in closet doors decorated with mother-cf-pearl inlay are worth examining closely. In each room, there are fireplaces and very elegant, double fountains in window recesses. The side of the building facing the courtyard is covered with tiles and has wide, decorated eaves.

After leaving the Apartment of the Crown Prince, the courtyard seen on the left is surrounded by the **Apartments of the Favorites** and on the north is the **Mabeyn of Sultan Abdülhamit I** (private apartment of the Sultan where he received the viziers). Although all of these apartments were built in the 18th century, sources indicate that during the reigns of previous sultans other importants buildings existed here.

The Golden Way: it is a narrow passageway which stretches from one end of the Harem to the other and connects the Courtyard of the Black Eunuchs and the terrace of the Sacred relics Section. Once, its walls were covered with tiles. It is claimed that during the Holy Days the sultans used to throw gold peices to the concubines as they walked down the passageway. Therefore, it is called the Golden Way.

There is a stairway leading to the rooms of the Kadın Efendis, their concubines and assistants.

A view of the tiles and the plaster windows in the Apartment of the Crown Prince.

LIFE IN THE HAREM

The most important and powerful woman in the Harem was the Valide Sultan, mother of the Sultan. Then came, in order, the Kadın Efendis (wives of the sultan), favorites, odalisks, supervisors and concubines, who were the least important. The concubines were chosen from minority groups, or were given as gifts to the sultans by governors, state leaders, or sisters of the sultans. They were brought from different lands, but most of them were from the Caucasus. For centuries, Circassian concubines were favored because of their beauty, talent and elegance.

When they first came to the palace, **the concubines** were give a medical examination and then, according to their beauty and talent, they were separated into groups. Each one was educated differently. The beautiful ones were assigned to the services of the sultans and the rest were trained to serve in different services of the Harem. Experienced concubines called Haznedars and Ustas (supervisors) were responsible for the education of the new concubines. Concubines were separated into three groups: Acemis (recruits), Ustas (supervisors) and Kalfas (assistants).

Harem, salon with fire place.

Roxelana, the wife of the Süleyman the Magnificent.

The number of concubines in the Harem varied with the reign of each sultan. In the beginning, there were few, but starting with Sultan Selim III, the number of concubines increased, and once there were as many as one thousand two hundred concubines in the Harem. All of them received satisfactory salaries and after a certain period of time, except for the odalisks, they could leave the palace. Some of them were married to high-ranking civil servants and their wedding expenses were paid for by the palace. Haznedars and Kalfas, after nine years service in the Harem, could leave the palace or ask the sultan's permission to get married.

The sultans could spent the night with any of the concubines they wanted. Yet, in the history of the Ottoman Empire, there have been many concubines who refused to spend a night with the sultan, in spite of his strong desires. Documents indicate that Abdülhamit I and Abdülhamit II were turned down by a few concubines. This negative attitude of the concubines in spite of the sultan's desire indicate that the sultans did not have indefinite freedom. In reality, it can only be interpreted as respect for women.

Sultans sometimes were not content with the women of the Harem only, but formed relationships with other women in Istanbul, whose fame they had heard of. In

The Harem, the bedroom of the Apartment of the Queen Mother.

order not to nurture jealousy among the women of the Harem, with the help of their sisters and the Grand Viziers, they kept these affairs secret. Sultan Mustafa III was involved in such an affair and letters about the relationship have been found.

In the Ottoman Palace, there were also sultans who were not fond of women. Osman III was one of them. The rumor is that, since he did not want to see any women, he used to wear shoes with large-headed nails in the soles while walking in the Harem, so the women would know he was coming and hide.

There are many stories about how and when a concubine attracted a sultan's attention and became his **odalisk.** In reality, the sultans encountered their concubines sometimes by coincidence, sometimes after hearing them sing, or even by creating circumstances. The concubine they wanted was prepared by the special people in charge. The women who spent even one night with a sultan became a **Privy Odalisk** and was given a private apartment and concubines to serve her. If she bore a child from a sultan, she became a **Kadın Efendi.**

If a sultan's first Privy Odalisk had a son, then she became the First Woman, and therefore, she usually became a **Valide Sultan** later. If a sultan did not like his concubine, he could marry her to one of his employees and get her out of the palace.

The wives of the sultans were called **Kadın Efendis** and there could be as many as eight. They were called the First Woman, Second Woman, etc. The favorites and odalisks who bore the sultan a son could become a kadın efendi if the sultan so desired.

Once they became a kadın efendi, they were given their private apartments and concubines. When their sons were old enough to become govenors in the provinces, they left Istanbul with their sons and lived in the provinces for a long time. Later this tradition was changed and they remained in the palace.

Upon the death of a sultan or his dethronement, his mother, wives, sisters and daughters were moved to the Old Palace. A kadın efendi could return to the palace only if her son became sultan and she became Valide Sultan.

Since the relationship between the sultans and their wives and odalisks was not always the same and sometimes the sultans were more interested in a new odalisk, jealousy and the resulting intrigues were quite prevalent in the Harem. Most of these intrigues stemmed from the desire of each kadın efendi to have her son become sultan.

If a sultan was weak or ineffectual, or a crown prince who ascended the throne was a child, then the Valide Sultan and his sisters became involved in the affairs of state. Usually, the wives of the sultans were quite respectful to each other. When they wanted to go out into the city, they took their assistants and concubines along with them. One of the black eunuchs always sat next to the driver of the carriage.

In the beginning of the 19th century, during the reign of Mahmut II, the women of the Harem started the tradition of going out on excursions and this tradition continued.

When they went out of the palace, the women wore a Çarşaf (over garment) or a Ferace (a light coat). In the palace, they used to hide their long braided hair in a Hotoz (headgear for women), or wore aigrettes or tiaras. The loose dresses they wore left open from the waist up and they wore belts with jeweled buckles. During the summer they wore silk dresses and in winter they wore dresses trimmed with fur. They also wore makeup and perfume.

Sultanahmet Mosque as seen from the Imperial Gate. __

NET.

PUBLICATION LIST

TURKEY (BN) (In English, French, German, Italian, Spanish, Dutch, Japanese ,Turkish)
ANCIENT CIVILIZATIONS AND RUINS OF TURKEY (En Anglais)
ISTANBUL (B) (In English, French, German, Italian, Spanish, Japonca, Turkish)
ISTANBUL (ORT) (In English, French, German, Italian, Spanish)
ISTANBUL (BN) (İngilizce, Fransızca, Almanca, Italian, Spanish, Japanese, Turkish)
MAJESTIC ISTANBUL (En Anglais, German)
TURKISH CARPETS (In English, French, German, Italian, Spanish, Japanese)
TURKISH CARPETS (En Anglais, German)
THE TOPKAPI PALACE (In English, French, German, Italian, Spanish, Japanese, Turkish)
HAGIA SOPHIA (In English, French, German, Italian, Spanish)
THE KARIYE MUSEUM (In English, French, German, Italian, Spanish)
ANKARA (In English, French, German, Italian, Spanish, Turkish)
CAPPADOCIA (In English, French, German, Italian, Spanish, Japanese, Turkish)
CAPPADOCIA (BN) (In English, French, German, Italian, Spanish, Dutch)
EPHESUS (In English, French, German, Italian, Spanish, Japanese, Turkish)
EPHESUS (BN) (In English, French, German, Italian, Spanish, Dutch)
APHRODISIAS (In English, French, German, Italian, Spanish, Turkish)
THE TURQUOISE COAST OF TURKEY (In English)
PAMUKKALE (In English, French, German, Italian, Spanish, Dutch, Japanese, Turkish)
PAMUKKALE (BN) (In English, French, German, Italian, Spanish, Turkish)
PERGAMON (In English, French, German, Italian, Spanish, Japanese)
LYCIA (AT) (In English, French, German)
KARIA (AT) (In English, French, German)
ANTALYA (BN) (In English, French, German, Italian, Dutch, Turkish)
PERGE (In English, French, German)
PHASELIS (In English, French, German, Turkish)
ASPENDOS (In English, French, German)
ALANYA (In English, French, German, Turkish)
The Capital of Urartu: VAN (In English, French, German)
TRABZON (In English, French, German, Turkish)
TURKISH COOKERY (In English, French, German, Italian, Spanish, Japanese, Turkish)
NASREDDIN HODJA (In English, French, German, Italian, Spanish, Japanese)
ANADOLU UYGARLIKLARI (Turkish)

Maps:

TURKEY (NET), TURKEY (ESR), TURKEY (West) TURKEY (South West), ISTANBUL, MARMARIS, ANTALYA-ALANYA, ANKARA, İZMİR, CAPPADOCIA

NET® BOOKSTORES

İSTANBUL GALLERİA BOOKSTORE:
Galleria Ataköy, Sahil Yolu, 34710 Ataköy Tel: (90-212) 559 09 50
İSTANBUL MERİT ANTIQUE BOOKSTORE:
Merit Antique Hotel İçi, Laleli Tel: (90-212) 513 93 00 - 513 64 31
İZMİR BOOKSTORE:
Cumhuriyet Bulvarı No: 142/B, 35210 Alsancak Tel: (90-232) 421 26 32